Mom, Share Your Life With Me...

Created by Kathleen Lashier

Copyright © 1993, Linkages

P.O. Box 821
Marshalltown, IA 50158
515-753-3670

Printed in the U.S.A.
G & R Publishing Co.
ISBN 1-56383-039-6

Distributed by:
CQ Products • 507 Industrial St. • Waverly, IA 50677
Phone: 800-887-4445 • Fax: 800-886-7496

Gift Page

To:

From:

Memory Journals for Special People

January 1
What was your day and date of birth?

January 2
Where were you born? Be specific.

January 3

Do you know any other circumstances of your birth (who was present, who delivered, etc.)?

January 4

If you have a childhood picture for me,
put it in this space.

January 5

Name your brothers and sisters and their years of birth.

January 6

What was your mother's full name?

January 7
What was your father's full name?

January 8

What was your mother's date and place of birth?

January 9

*What was your father's date
and place of birth?*

January 10

*Tell a family nickname that you had.
How did you get it?*

January 11
Tell of any other nicknames in your family.

January 12
What did your father do for a living?

January 13

Did your mother work outside the home?

January 14

Name the towns you lived in before you were 20.

January 15
*Name the childhood addresses
you remember.*

January 16

Tell a fond memory of your Grandpa.

January 17

Tell a fond memory of your Grandma.

January 18
Tell about a favorite Aunt.

January 19

Tell about a favorite Uncle.

January 20

Did any relatives ever live with you?

January 21

Relate an experience or memory of a cousin.

January 22

When you needed punishment as a child, which parent corrected you, and how?

January 23

Tell about the naughtiest thing you ever did. If you got caught, describe the consequences.

January 24
Who was the President when you were born?

January 25

At what age did you first vote and for whom did you cast your first Presidential vote?

January 26
*Did you ever see a President or
Vice-President in person?*

January 27

Did you ever have an imaginary friend?

January 28

What did you and your brothers or sisters fight about the most?

January 29

What was the dumbest stunt ever pulled by you and a brother or sister?

January 30

Tell about the worst winter storm that you can remember as a child.

January 31

What did you use to go sledding down a hill in the snow?

February 1

What extras did you use for your snowman's face, buttons, arms, hat, etc?

February 2
Do you have any ice skating memories to share?

February 3

Share a memory about a weather-related school cancellation.

February 4

Do you have any knowledge of the origins of your family name?

February 5
What were you doing to first smash a finger?

February 6

Who was the most famous person you ever met as a child?

February 7
Tell about a big fib you told.

February 8

Tell about someone who had a big influence over your life.

February 9

*Tell of a nickname given to you
by friends or classmates.
How did you get it?*

February 10
What was your favorite meal as a child?

February 11
Who was your first boyfriend?

February 12

Tell about the Valentine Day festivities at your school.

February 13

Tell about a special valentine

you once gave.

February 14

*Tell about a special valentine
you once received.*

February 15
Tell about your first date.

February 16
Tell about your first kiss.

February 17

Tell about your first favorite TV shows.

February 18
Tell about family reunions in your childhood.

February 19

What do you remember as your favorite subject in school?

February 20

*What do you remember as your least
favorite school subject?*

February 21

What is the biggest problem you remember having in Grade School?

February 22

What is the biggest problem you remember having in Jr. High school?

February 23

What is the biggest problem you remember having in Sr. High school?

February 24

Describe a place you liked to go to be alone.

February 25

Tell of a place that you discovered or built as a "haven" for your gang.

February 26

Tell about a favorite "hang out" place for you and your friends in Jr. or Sr. High.

February 27
Tell about the best pet you ever had.

February 28
Tell about other pets you had.

March 1

Tell about being in a school play or program.

March 2

Tell about a school principal you remember.

March 3

Did you ever pretend to be sick as an excuse to stay home from school?

March 4

*Do you have a good story
about yourself cussing?*

March 5

Tell about how you spent your Saturdays during the school year.

March 6

Tell about how you spent your Sundays.

March 7

*What was the naughtiest or meanest thing
you remember doing in school?
Were there consequences?*

March 8

When on car trips,
did you play car games?

March 9

What was your favorite radio program?

March 10

What was your favorite movie as a youth? Why?

March 11

Did kids ever tease you? About what?

March 12

Tell of a difficult school essay or term paper assignment.

March 13
Tell about your first smoke.

March 14

Do you remember your first pizza?

March 15

If you went to college, tell which college you chose and why.

March 16

Tell your major and how you chose it.

March 17

Did people wear green on St. Patrick's Day?

March 18

Do you have any other memories of St. Patrick's Day as a youth?

March 19

If you ever hitch-hiked, explain.

March 20

What do you remember as your favorite time of year? Why?

March 21
Describe some household chores you had as a child.

March 22
Describe some outside chores.

March 23
Which chore did you dislike the most?

March 24

What bones have you broken and how?

March 25
Did you ever need stitches?

March 26

Do you have any other good stories about being injured?

March 27
Tell of a childhood illness.

March 28

Tell about an experience at the doctor's or dentist's.

March 29

Name your best school chums.

March 30

What were some crazy names or nicknames in your school?

March 31
Tell about a practical joke or prank you played on a person.

April 1

Do you have a good April Fool's Day story?

April 2

Tell about a practical joke or prank someone played on you?

April 3

As a child, what did you want to be when you grew up?

April 4

Did you ever make a kite? How? Tell about your kite-flying experiences.

April 5
Did you ever feel a hatred for another person? Explain.

April 6
Have you ever hunted, or tried to capture a wild animal?

April 7
Did you ever try to adopt a wild animal?

April 8
Make up a limerick about yourself.

April 9

Make up a limerick about me.

April 10

Relate a favorite spring memory.

April 11
Did your Mom or Dad ever find something you had hidden?

April 12

Share a memory of going to church as you were growing up.

April 13
Share a memory about a church social activity.

(If the following Easter topics do not apply, please share your special Holiday memories and traditions.)

April 14

Tell about an Easter Egg hunt.

April 15

Tell about any other Easter traditions.

April 16

Did you ever have a recurring dream as a child?

April 17
When you played make-believe, what did you pretend?

April 18

Tell about the best birthday present you ever received.

April 19

Tell about any sports you played in Junior or Senior High.

April 20
Did you ever write something that you were really proud of?

April 21
What is the best book you ever read as a child?

April 22

What is the biggest physical problem you had to deal with?

April 23

Did you have any superstitions?

April 24
Where were your best hide-and-seek places?

April 25

Tell about the first time you were ever behind the wheel of a car.

April 26
Did you ever take anything that wasn't yours?

April 27

What did you do with it?
Did you get caught?

April 28

Do you have a story about a big surprise?

April 29

What childhood fear do you remember?

April 30
Tell about a May Day tradition.

May 1

What were May Baskets made of and what did they contain?

May 2
How much do you remember paying for an ice cream cone?

May 3
Did you have a treehouse?

May 4
Were you ever bitten by a dog?

May 5

Did your Mother ever make a special gift for you?

May 6
Tell a favorite memory of your mother.

May 7

Tell about some good advice your mother gave you.

May 8

Relate your family Mother's Day traditions.

May 9
*Do you remember any childhood
songs or rhymes?*

May 10
*Name some popular hit songs
from your youth.*

May 11
What was your favorite singing group or band?

May 12

Tell a favorite singer and a song that he/she sang?

May 13
*What kind of dances did
you do as a youth?*

May 14
Tell about the first dance you ever went to.

May 15

Tell about your high school prom or formal dance.

May 16

Describe your military experience or that of someone in your family.

May 17

Share a memory involving a war during your childhood or youth.

May 18

Share another memory involving a war during childhood or youth.

May 19

If you have another photograph of your childhood to share, place it here.

May 20

Tell about your graduation exercises or traditions.

May 21
What year did you graduate from high school?

May 22

How many students were in your high school? In your graduating class?

May 23

Tell of someone you envied and why.

May 24

Did you have homework?

May 25
Describe a very proud moment in your childhood.

May 26

Tell about Memorial Day traditions during your youth.

May 27

Share a special memory of Memorial Day.

May 28

Did you play a musical instrument?

May 29

Tell of the closest friend you had during your childhood.

May 30

Is there anything you have now that you have kept from your childhood?

May 31

Do you have any good bathtime stories?

June 1

Tell about a strange person that lived in your town.

June 2
What was the funniest name or nickname in your town?

June 3

Did you ever sleep under the stars?

June 4

Tell about hot dog or marshmallow roasting.

June 5

Did you ever go on a camp out?
Tell about it.

June 6

Did you ever go on a snipe hunt?

June 7

What food did you learn to cook or prepare first as a youth?

June 8
Share a horse-riding story.

June 9

What was your first job?

June 10
How much did you get paid?

June 11

Tell about any other paying jobs you held as a youth.

June 12

Were you ever chased by some animal?

June 13

If you were ever in a parade, tell about it.

June 14

Tell another memory about a parade.

June 15

Share a childhood memory about a death that affected you.

June 16
Relate your happiest memory as a youth.

June 17

How did you learn to swim?

June 18
Where did you go swimming?

June 19

Tell a favorite memory of your father.

June 20

Tell about some good advice your father gave you.

June 21

Did your father ever make a special gift for you?

June 22

Did you have a special nature place where you went to explore?

June 23

Did you ever go skinny-dipping?

June 24

Did you ever make mud pies?

June 25

*Did you go barefoot in the summer?
If so, relate an experience about
stepping on something.*

June 26

Describe a few of the favorite hair styles of your youth.

June 27
Tell about a bike you had.

June 28

As a youth, did you ever learn any sewing, stitching, or needlework?

June 29

Did you ever have or make a swing?

June 30

Tell about seeing something you thought was very beautiful.

July 1
Describe an outside game you made up.

July 2
Describe an inside game you made up.

July 3

What kind of fireworks did people have when you were a youth?

July 4

*Tell about Independence Day
traditions of your childhood.*

July 5

Do you have a special July 4th that you remember most?

July 6

Did you ever go to carnivals or amusement parks? Where?

July 7

What kinds of rides and games were there? How much did they cost?

July 8

Tell about any State Fair or County Fair experiences.

July 9

Tell about going to a circus or chautauqua.

July 10
Tell any favorite summertime memory.

July 11
Did you go fishing in your childhood?

July 12

Tell about your biggest or best catch.

July 13

Do you remember having a favorite candy? How much did it cost?

July 14

Do you remember having a favorite snack that you made at home?

July 15

Share a memory about going on a picnic.

July 16
What kinds of party games or party activities were popular?

July 17
Share a memory involving a heatwave or drought.

July 18
What did you do to stay cool?

July 19

What was your favorite holiday
of the year? Why?

July 20
Share a birthday party memory.

July 21

Tell about the neatest shoes you ever owned as a youth.

July 22

Share a memory about a power outage.

July 23
Relate a memory involving a flood or cloudburst.

July 24

Relate a memory of a tornado, hurricane, or destructive wind.

July 25

What memories do you have of lightning or thunder during your childhood?

July 26

Share a special memory about riding in a boat.

July 27
Tell about a family vacation trip.

July 28
Share the best vacation experience you can recall.

July 29

Share the most unpleasant vacation experience you can recall.

July 30

Do you have any other memories about a river, lake, or beach to share?

July 31
Tell a memory about riding on a ferry, bus, train, or plane.

August 1

*If you were to return to your youth,
what would you do differently?*

August 2
Describe your childhood home & neighborhood.

August 3
Tell about going to a summer camp.

August 4

Tell of an experience climbing a mountain or big hill.

August 5

Tell a memory about having company at your house, or of a family party.

August 6

Tell about board games and card games you played as a youth.

August 7

Did your mom or dad have a favorite remedy for what ailed you?

August 8
Share an experience about poison ivy or poison weed.

August 9
What was your best talent?

August 10

Tell about a time when you got lost.

August 11
Did you ever play in the
sprinkler or hose?

August 12
Tell about being stung by a bee or wasp.

August 13

Did you have any favorite family songs that you sang together?

August 14
Tell about your bedroom.

August 15

Share a memory of staying overnight with a friend.

August 16

If you ever ran away from home, tell about it.

August 17

Do you remember being really curious about something?

August 18

Share your childhood experiences with roller skates.

August 19

Did you ever experience home sickness?

August 20

*Did you ever make a purchase
that you later regretted?*

August 21

Share an early experience with make-up.

August 22

Tell about a favorite doll, teddy bear, or other stuffed toy.

August 23
Tell about another favorite toy.

August 24

Did you have to abide by a curfew as a youth?

August 25

*If you ever had a hero, tell who.
Tell why.*

August 26
Describe how you used the phone to call a friend.

August 27

Did you ever have a fire in your home or accidentally catch something on fire?

August 28
Tell about going to box socials or pot lucks.

August 29

Tell about an incident when you were very angry with your mom or dad.

August 30

Tell about an incident when your mom or dad was very angry with you.

August 31

Share a memory involving an outhouse.

September 1

Do you remember any Labor Day traditions of your youth?

September 2

Do you have a memory involving V.J. Day?

September 3
What do you remember about your first day of school?

September 4
Tell about your school year calendar.

September 5
Tell about a school bully.

September 6
What do you remember doing at recess?

September 7

Tell about the playground equipment at your grade school.

September 8

Did your parents ever make you wear something stupid to school?

September 9

Tell about who you thought was the smartest kid in school and why.

September 10

Tell about who you thought was the dumbest kid in school and why.

September 11

Tell about the naughtiest kid in school.

September 12
Tell about a teacher's pet.

September 13

Name the schools that you went to.

September 14
What was your most embarrassing school moment?

September 15
What teacher did you dislike the most?
Why?

September 16

Did you ever have a crush on a teacher?

September 17
Who was the best teacher you ever had?
Why?

September 18
Describe your typical school day outfit.

September 19

If you were ever in a fight, tell about it.

September 20
Tell about your worst report card.

September 21

What is the worst trick that you remember a student playing on a teacher?

September 22

What is the worst thing that you remember a teacher doing to a student?

September 23

How did you get to and from school?

September 24

*Do you remember
a special school custodian?*

September 25

What were your school colors?

September 26

What was your school mascot?

September 27

Tell about a memorable birthday cake.

September 28

Did you ever have a "good friend" who did something mean to you?

September 29

How did your school observe Homecoming?

September 30

Do you have any special Homecoming experiences to relate?

October 1

Did your High School have cheerleaders?
What did they wear?

October 2

Can you recite any of your school cheers?

October 3
Tell about any other extra-curricular activities.

October 4

Do you have a good piece of advice for me?

October 5

Do you have any special memories about raking and burning leaves, or mowing the lawn?

October 6

If you ever played in the leaves,
tell about it.

October 7
What allowance did you get?

October 8
Did you have to earn it?

October 9

What was your most prized possession as a child?

October 10

What is the strangest thing you ever saw in the sky?

October 11

Relate a story about a mouse in the house.

October 12

Share a memory about a bat in the house.

October 13

Did you ever have any other strange animal in the house?

October 14

Do you remember the first movie you ever saw? Who starred in it?

October 15

Do you have a good school pants-wetting story?

October 16

Tell about pulling or losing a baby tooth.

October 17

Did you ever lose something really important to you?

October 18

Did you ever lose or break something that belonged to someone else?

October 19

Was an injustice ever done to you?

October 20
Share a favorite fall memory.

October 21

Do you have a story about standing up against odds for something you really believed in?

October 22
What is the farthest you ever ran or walked?

October 23
Did you ever pick apples?

October 24
If you had a watch, tell about it.

October 25

What hobbies or collections did you have as a youth?

October 26
Share a memory about being very scared.

October 27

Tell a story about a time when you dressed up in a costume.

October 28

Did you ever tell ghost stories?

October 29

Do you have a good ghost or haunted house story to relate?

October 30
What did people do at Halloween?

October 31

*Do you have a special
Halloween memory?*

November questions will deal with your courtship, marriage, and my arrival in the world.

November 1

Tell about how you first knew my father.

November 2

Tell about your first date with him.

November 3
What qualities first attracted you to him?

November 4
Tell about how my dad proposed marriage to you.

November 5

If you have a picture taken during your courtship to share, place it here.

November 6
When and where were you married?

November 7
What did you wear?

November 8
Who performed the ceremony?
Who stood up with you?

November 9

Tell about any other circumstances of your wedding day.

November 10
Did you go on a honeymoon?

November 11

Do you have an Armistice Day memory?

November 12
Tell about where you lived when first married.

November 13

What was your job at the time?

November 14

What qualities in my dad did you try unsuccessfully to change?

November 15

Tell about the most serious problem or challenge you faced during your early years of marriage.

November 16

Tell the full names, birthdays, and birthplaces of all of your children.

November 17
Tell about the day I was born.

November 18

How did you choose my name?

November 19

What other names did you consider for me?

November 20

Who was the President when I was born?

November 21

If you have a baby picture of me to share, place it here.

November 22

What were you doing when John F. Kennedy was assassinated?

November 23
What was the address of my first childhood home?

November 24

What do you remember most about my first month of life?

November 25
What were my other childhood addresses?

November 26

Share your favorite funny story of me as a child.

November 27
Share a favorite Thanksgiving memory.

November 28

Tell about the Thanksgiving traditions of your youth. What foods were on your Thanksgiving table?

November 29
Tell your all-time favorites:

Food-

Book-

Movie-

November 30

More favorites:

TV Show-

Song-

Color-

December 1

More favorites:

Bible verse-

Pastime-

December 2

As a youth, who was your favorite movie star? Why?

December 3

Do you have another good piece of advice for me?

December 4
Were you ever in a life-threatening situation?

December 5

*Did you ever have a bad experience
with a haircut or a permanent?*

December 6

Do you have any knowledge of how your first name was chosen?

December 7
Do you have a Pearl Harbor Day memory?

December 8

Tell about your favorite store to browse in as a child.

December 9
What did you like to look at there?

December 10

Tell about something you built, designed, or made as a youth.

December 11

Were you ever in a church or school Christmas or Holiday pageant?

(If the following Christmas topics do not apply, please share your special Holiday memories and traditions.)

December 12

When did you put up your Christmas tree? Where did you get them?

December 13
How did you decorate your trees?

December 14

Did you hang a Christmas stocking?

December 15

Did your Grandpa or Grandma ever make gifts for you? What?

December 16

Tell about the neatest present you remember giving to your Mom.

December 17

Tell about the neatest present you remember giving to your Dad.

December 18

Tell about the best Christmas present you ever received, as a child.

December 19

Tell about the worst Christmas present you ever received, as a child.

December 20

Tell about your experiences with Santa Claus.

December 21

Do you remember a "best" Christmas of childhood?

December 22

Tell about Holiday celebrations at a relative's house during your childhood.

December 23

Did your family go to a special church service at Christmas? Tell about it.

December 24

Tell about the most memorable gifts you have given me.

December 25

*Tell about the most memorable gifts
I have given you.*

December 26

Share any other Christmas memory.

December 27

Do you remember celebrating any special wedding anniversaries of your parents or grandparents?

December 28
Is there anything else you would like me to know about your childhood?

December 29

Is there anything else that you would like me to know about <u>my</u> childhood?

December 30

Did you ever make New Year's resolutions?

December 31

What special memories do you have of New Year's Eve or New Year's Day?